T0208720

Other Books by the Author

Biff and Becka's Springtime Escapades

Biff and Becka's Stupendous Vacation

Biff and Becka's Splendiferous Christmas

Elaine's Kitchen Cookbook

Journal Gems: Nuggets from My Heart to Yours

www.elainebeachy.com
elainesplace4@verizon.net (e-mail)

Rhyme and Reason

A COLLECTION OF POETRY AND SHORT STORIES

ELAINE BEACHY

WESTBOW
PRESS®
A DIVISION OF THOMAS NELSON
& ZONDERVAN

Unless otherwise indicated, scripture is taken from the King James Version of the Bible.

Scripture marked NIV is taken from The Holy Bible, New International Version®, NIV® Copyright © 1973, 1978, 1984, 2011 by Biblica, Inc.® Used by permission. All rights reserved worldwide.

WestBow Press books may be ordered through booksellers or by contacting:

WestBow Press
A Division of Thomas Nelson & Zondervan
1663 Liberty Drive
Bloomington, IN 47403
www.westbowpress.com
1 (866) 928-1240

ISBN: 978-1-9736-4931-1 (sc)
ISBN: 978-1-9736-4930-4 (hc)
ISBN: 978-1-9736-4932-8 (e)

Library of Congress Control Number: 2018914938

Print information available on the last page.

WestBow Press rev. date: 01/08/2019

Dedication Page

Thanks to God my Father, my Lord and Savior, Jesus Christ, and the Holy Spirit for inspiration and the joy of writing. May Your kingdom come, and Your will be done on Earth, as it is in Heaven.

To my dear husband, Dave, whose love and encouragement means the world to me; to my beloved children, Douglas, Debra, and Darren, and to my grandchildren, Alissa, Nicole, Caleb, and Noelle;

To my mother, Elva, and the memory of my father Edwin;

To my brothers: Stanley, Sanford, Marlin, and George, their spouses and families;

Thank you for your love and support! You have all shaped my life for the better, in one way or another.

Thanks also to the editors and designers at WestBow Press for helping me get this book published.

Table of Contents

SHORT STORIES

Preface

There's something about writing poetry that satisfies a creative sense in me. In 1993 I began to transfer all my scattered poetry into one book, so I wouldn't lose it. I didn't arrange them by date, but just wrote them down as I came across them. Sometimes the emotion of what I feel is best expressed in poetry rather than in prose. I hope you enjoy the variety of my poems.

> Some are free verse, others rhyme;
> Some were written at a time
> Of deep emotion in my mind.
>
> Some are happy, some are sad.
> Some make you think, some make you glad.
>
> Some are songs, or just for fun.
> Some are sermons in a poem.
>
> Some are short, some are long;
> Some bare my soul when I felt wrong.
> Please enjoy and pass this on!

Included in my collection of short stories is a piece of biblical fiction titled "Man of Honor" about what life could have been like for Joseph and Mary when she was found to be with child by the Holy Spirit. Joseph and Mary were real people, living in a community among family and friends. We tend to read the story in the Bible from a faraway perspective without imagining how things could very likely have been for them.

I didn't realize until I had my manuscript done that I began my book with the free-verse poem "Paradise Lost," and ended my book with a descriptive narrative titled "A Touch of Eden." It's like I came full circle and God tied my book with a bow.

Thank you for reading my collections, and may God bless you!

Paradise Lost

What spoiler of Eden
Still spoils today
As he did that day
Long ago?
From whence did evil spring?
What prompted pride—
That alien force in the heavenlies?
Sin was found in Lucifer
As he walked before his God.

What misery was wrought
In God's beloved earth
As evil heart, in revenge,
Was set against God's creation
By him who was cast
From heaven?

With hateful eye,
He viewed humankind,
Determined to wound
The heart of God
By enticing His creation
Into alliance against the truth.

"Did God really say?"[1]
Is the arrow shot
At us today
As it was that day
Eden died.

---

[1] Genesis 3:1

Reunion

Close-knit to God
In cool of day,
Mankind once ruled with joy.
One hand out-stretched,
One simple act—
To pluck forbidden fruit—,
Once-glorious couple
Relinquished authority
Over earth
That day they fell. Then,
Earth's ruthless master
Bound the once-free
Heart of mankind.
Cruel taskmaster, he;
Pitiless and diabolical!

Love and mercy wept
At painful estrangement
Between God and His beloved.
We hid our faces,
Unable to meet His gaze.
We did not understand
He'd set His love on us,
His arms reaching, aching,
Like a parent's
Whose hostage child
Cannot come home.

So, God clothed Himself
In form as a man
And lived among us
For a time.

He, last Adam,
Refusing to yield
To serpentine splendor,
Doing good where He walked,
Compassion written on His face,
Showed us the Father.

God placed on Him,
The sinless Son,
The sins of everyone;
And He made payment
For those
Who could not pay
The price of peace.

What perfect horror
As sinless Son
Gave Himself
To be made sin
In cruelest death
With our sinfulness!

No sin His own,
Yet our sin was laid
To His account
So that we,
Who had no holiness,
Could have righteousness
Laid to ours.

What great exchange
Was made!
With resurrection power,
Love and mercy leapt

At joyful reunion
Of God and His people!
We met His gaze—
We understood—
His love reached out
And brought us home.

For Now

"He is Alpha and Omega
Beginning and End,
The First and Last,"[2]
The past, present, and future.
"In the beginning was the Word;
The Word was with God
And the Word was God."[3]
He made the world,
Made me in His image.
All life bears the imprint
And orderly design
Of God.
"In Him, all things consist."[4]
The sun rises and sets
In perpetual warmth,
Bearing testimony
Of His faithfulness.
In the heart of everyone
Lies the seed of faith
To believe in Him.

But my mind
Stands on tiptoe,
Searching in vain
To know the birthplace
Of God.
I climb to the apex
And strain to see
Beyond the void

---

[2] Revelation 20:13
[3] John 1:1
[4] Colossians 1:17

That greets me there.
Why is there God?
Who put Him where He is?
Did He make Himself?
Impossible!

At the pinnacle of wonder
I find a black void,
A secret quiet,
Territory impenetrable.
I draw back into the light.
Ah, someday I will know
As I enter His heaven.
But here, I content myself
To bask in His faithfulness.
This I know:
He has touched my heart
And is my friend,
Having spoken to me
Through His word,
Telling me things
I need to know
For now.

Agape Love

Before I drew my first breath,
You knew me.
Before I said, "I love You,"
You already loved me.
Before I walked one step toward You,
You had walked to Calvary for me.
Before I said, "I'm sorry,"
You had already forgiven me.
Before I called,
You answered.
Before I walked away from You,
You had already welcomed me back.

Self-Image

Upon the easel still it stands,
A form, unfinished, new.
The canvas wet, and not yet filled;
The details also few.

She sees the frame bent out of shape,
And, also, colors bland.
With loving heart and eyes, He sees
His image in His hands.

I see a painting, rare and bright,
Which skillful fingers wrought;
The price of which no one could pay—
The blood of Jesus bought!

America the Needy

Like the teen whose heart rebellious
Against the parent's hand is raised,
Going his own way, now dismal,
Loathes to seek parental aid,

So our country, heart rebellious,
Turned her heart from God alone
To free love, libbers, drugs, abortion,
New Age crystals—hapless stones.

With her hands out-stretched for answers,
Attacked and wounded, blinded, sore,
She relucts to find salvation
From the One she so abhorred.

Struggle on, then, one rebellious;
Pile on laws, and legislate!
Watch your cities, towns and families
Buckle under such a fate.

With His heart of mercy aching,
God waits patiently to see
When her eyes will turn upon Him,
So that He might set her free.

Who'll repair the crumbling moorings?
Who will shout the watchman's cry?
Who calls out, "Awake, you sleeper!
Don your armor! To the fray!"

Is it not the godly-minded
Who for long were trodden down,
Those with faith in God, united,
Who restore our country's crown?

Heartstrings

From diapers, bottles, Playskool toys,
To crayons, pencils, books,
My children grew from year to year;
Time also changed their looks.

How small they seemed, how innocent,
How fresh their little minds.
My heartstrings cried that day at school
I first left them behind.

As time marched on so callously,
My heart could plainly see
My little children, bit by bit,
Had grown away from me.

Is not the parent's call to be
The help to train the young—
Develop wings and strength to fly—
Be on their own, and strong?

Yes, this I know. All will be well
With heaven on their side.
They stand up tall and face the world;
My heartstrings swell with pride!

Wedding Day

How tall she stands,
How regal-robed,
My lovely grown-up girl!
The rosebuds in
Her bride's bouquet
Are mixed with tiny pearls.

The gleaming satin
Of her gown
Is pedestal for grace
That shines from eyes
So dark and wide
To blush that tints her face.

From dreamy veil
Of purity,
To base of snow-white shoes,
The best part is
My daughter's heart.
It's just as lovely, too!

Tie-Breaker

Behind a filmy veil of lace,
Her rosebud-gentle smile
Reflects the joy within her heart
As she walks down the aisle.

How sweet and fair, how purely-clad,
Our lovely daughter stands,
Awaiting her beloved's pledge
To ring her dainty hand.

A tender look, a gentle touch,
As hands become entwined.
Another's trust she enters now;
Our care she leaves behind.

How bitter-sweet the poignant taste
To unfamiliar tongue,
As parent ties dissolve with tears.
Yet, we have gained a son!

Pain

The stream runs deep
Of ties so true.
As sad heart aches,
I think of you.

The days of mirth
And friendship shared
Are sorely missed,
My family fair.

Remember when—
O wistful thought—
Our hearts were one,
As Jesus taught?

Estranged

Who came between?
Who led astray?
Who cast a spell?
Who feigned "the way"?

What demons sly?
What words they said?
What 'witched your eyes?
What turned your head?

When that one urged,
When demons lied,
When "Shun those preachers!"
When gladness died. . .

Where days of joy?
Where love for truth?
Where loving arms?
Where smile that soothes?

Why closed the door?
Why silence loud?
Why paths avoided?
Why deaf to God?

How devils glee!
How built the web!
How shunned old friends!
How blindly led!

Don't shut me out—
Please speak to me.
You're flesh and blood—
My family.

Restored

God came between
The pain and me
And helped my longing
Soul to see
The prayer of faith
Would win the day
And would restore us
All the way.

For years we prayed;
And then one day
Out of the blue
The call that came
Restored our family
Once again!
All thanks and praise
To Jesus's name!

Perspective

We've been born from above
To a kingdom of love.
Our home is up there,
But while we are here,
Let's do things
As they are done there.
God said in His word
What we bind on the earth
Will also be bound up there.

There's no sickness, no sadness,
Hatred or madness—
Let's not allow it here.
There's no bitterness, envy,
Or unholy anger,
Discontentment, resentment up there.
Let's not allow it here.

Let us lift up our brother,
Be kind to each other—
That's the way that they do it up there.
The kingdom of God is within us;
We are ruled by this kingdom of love.
There's one holy family
Up there and down here,
Joined by the Spirit of God.

As they praise Him up there,
We'll praise Him down here,
And live out of this kingdom of love.
Then one of these days,
We'll move from down here

When God calls us to meet Him up there.
May we hear these words:
"Well done, faithful son,
You've done it down there
The way it's done here."[5]

He's Changing Me

Have you ever thought it's hard to live a holy life?
Have you ever felt it's just too hard to do?
Always hoping you will please the Lord above enough?
Then, my friend, I want to sing this song for you.

Chorus:
He's changing me, He's changing me,
A brand-new life He's given me,
And he takes away the efforts of my flesh, oh yes, He does!
He's changing me, He's changing me,
A brand-new life He's given me,
And He's given me a glad, rejoicing heart.

I rejoice in all the goodness of my Savior,
And not in the works that my own will can do.
Now I rest in what He's done, not in my efforts;
That's the only way that God will see me through.

I have entered into rest—the rest that Jesus gives;
I have laid aside the efforts of my pride;
Now I know that I am holy by what Jesus did,
Not by trying to be good all of my life.

It pleases God if I just rest in Jesus' work for me,
And receive His goodness like it was my own;
No more shrinking from His presence—He's forgiven me!
He says, "Come, now boldly come, before My throne."[6]

---

[6] Hebrews 4:16

A Prayer Song

For covenant relationship, I thank You.
Works of law can never make me free!
Earning favors, working, being all through,
The power of God, through Jesus, lives in me.

Chorus:
Fill me with your resurrection power;
Holy Spirit, fill me with your love!
Cause me to be full this very hour
Of wonder-working power from above.

I hide Your Word within my heart, Lord Jesus,
To do and not just hear is my desire.
You are my example, precious Jesus;
To minister, I need the Spirit's fire.

Burn fully in my heart, O Holy Spirit,
Burn out the sin that robs me of my power
To live in light and total consecration.
Burn full flame in me, now from this hour.

You've place me here, a person for Your glory,
I am a king and priest right where I stand!
You've given me a mountain-moving story
To share with everyone here in this land.

(I sang this song with my accordion the day I was guest speaker
in the spring of 1985 at Women's Aglow Fellowship in Somerset,
Pennsylvania.)

My Dearest Dad

My dearest dad, don't think you're old;
You're only forty-seven!
And all the things you've done for me
Have made my life a haven.

Thank you more than I can say
For your prayers for me.
You've always tried to teach me right,
That I God's child might be.

Thank you for the altar time
Where we'd read each day.
And after you explained God's word,
The family knelt to pray.

Thanks for tea sets, dolls and books,
For hayrides, wiener roasts and such;
For picnics, parties, taste-freeze:
These things all meant so much.

I never will forget the time
You had trouble with your heart.
I'm thankful that God spared your life
And didn't have to part.

To me, you are the greatest dad
A girl could ever have.
And at a time when I would spend,
You taught me how to save.

Now I have my own sweet home,
And you're a grandpa, too!
I'm proud to tell my little boy
That his grandpa is you!

So, thanks, in many million ways
For my Christian home.
May your days be filled with joy
For many years to come!

My Dearest Mom

My dearest Mom, I'm glad you're mine.
I sure would want no other!
When God made you, He surely made
The bestest kind of mother!

When I think of loving deeds,
I don't know where to start!
But best of all, the Christ you loved,
To me you did impart.

I have here, within my heart
A very tender place
For my sweetest, kindest mother,
With her loving face.

You taught me when I was eleven,
To iron Dad's white shirts.
And when the boys came tramping in,
Oh, how we'd hate that dirt!

You taught me how to wash and cook,
To clean and make the beds.
The things you taught me way back then,
A guiding ray now sheds.

I learned, when very young,
To mix up pies and batter.
And when I'd drop an egg or cup,
You said, "It doesn't matter."

Remember how, when Georgie came,
You thought a girl 'twould be?
You washed and pressed the little clothes
That had been worn by me.

You and I, we've been so close,
You've seemed to fill the space
For that Sis I always wanted.
Yes, you took that place.

So, thanks, dear Mom, for everything;
And now that you're Grandma,
May I teach my boy the right
Like you and dear Grandpa.

Yes, you and Dad have always been
The sweetest parents ever.
And may we have a lot more time
To spend good times together!

Silent Call

Why am I here?
Why do I do?
The truth is in
God's holy book.
He longs for me
To be His friend;
He loves me first,
Calls me by name.

Day into night,
Night into day;
Day after day
I breathe a breath
And silent call
To find the meaning
Of it all.

Why am I here?
Why do I do?
The truth is in
God's holy book.
He really wants me
For a friend.
He loved me first—
Called me by name.

Darwin Jive

Evolution, Darwin spawned;
God created,
New day dawned.
In God's image
Man is made;
Fish and apes
Don't make the grade.

Cro-magnon man,
The theory goes,
Could barely walk
Upon his toes.
Ten billion years
Or more, they say,
It took to make
Our man today.

Evolution, Darwin spawned;
God created,
New day dawned.
In God's image
Man is made
Don't mess with truth—
God's center stage!

The Witness

Sin of man abounds,
Truth is fallen to the ground,
Spreads the misery around.
I can't look away.

Behind my mask I hide,
Shielding truth I know inside,
Afraid to go against the tide.
I hang my head in shame.

A distant cross appears,
I see the Christ through tears.
The image ever nears;
I look at Him.

Sin of man abounds,
Truth is fallen to the ground,
Spreads the misery around.
I find my voice
And shout aloud,
Repent and look up
To the Lord!

Unborn

Look around and see.
Who's concerned for me?

Creator of my inmost being,
When I was woven
In the dark
Your eyes saw
My unformed body.
"All the days
Ordained for me
Were written in Your book
Before one of them
Came to be."[7]

Look around and see.
Who's concerned for me?

Unborn member of the race,
Print of God upon my face.
Tiny hands and tiny feet,
Innocent and sweet.

Look around and see.
Who's concerned for me?

---

[7] Psalm 139:16, NIV

Hallowed, eagle's nest;
Spotted owl is blessed.
Blue whale out at sea,
Favored more than me.

Look around and see.
Who's concerned for me?

Rescue me!

We Weep

Let the cry begin!
This is a sin!
How can we claim
To not feel the shame?
Do we not share the blame:
God's people divided
By political parties
With whom we have sided,
When we should have united
With truth?
Yes!

For
Tiny nose that will never smell,
Tiny ears that will never hear,
Tiny feet that will never walk,
Tiny eyes that will never see,
Tiny arms that will never hug,
Tiny hands that will never be useful,
We weep.

Where's justice for these
Most helpless of all?
Please turn and heed
The Holy One's call!

Legacy of Love

Patiently, he waits as Mother arranges us
Around the table; and when we're seated,
He asks that we sing together.
Eyes closed, hands clasped together,
He begins to sing: "God is so good,
God is so good, He's so good to me."
And then he prays a blessing
On his children, grandchildren,
And on the food,
Praying in hushed tones
To the Savior he loves so much.

He slowly reaches for another piece of celery
As we still sit around the table
Busily chattering like noisy magpies.
(Mother has finally seated herself
To enjoy her piece of pie
After serving all the rest of us.)
His blue plaid flannel shirt
Faintly echoes the softness of his smile
As he reaches over to stroke Mother's arm.
His heart, too, is warm and soft
Like that flannel shirt.

At the door, his tender "Good-bye"
And warm hug is coupled with
"God bless you, my daughter."
I feel as loved and accepted by him
As if I were his own daughter.
Little do I know it is the last time
I will look into his "Jesus eyes,"
The tender-hearted eyes of a soul

We called Irvin.
I am richer for having known him,
And I am doubly blessed to have his son
As my husband.

The Shaking of Nations

The Iron Curtain fell,
The Berlin Wall came down,
Soviet Union is no more.
Gorbacheve is out,
Yeltsin is in—
For how long?
Where has Communism gone?
Where have the Kremlin police gone?
Their whole army?
Ideas don't die,
They are spirit.
They have come to America
In diabolical swiftness.
What is the meaning
Of this cultural upheaval
Being fueled in epic proportions
From sixteen-hundred Pennsylvania Avenue,
Bent on propagating
The acceptance of homosexuality,
Abortion, lesbianism,
Radical feminism,
Big Brother government?
God, help us!

Written in the spring of 1993 after Bill Clinton took office.

The Picture

As she handed me the picture
They had treasured many years,
Emotions stirred within my soul
As I blinked back the tears.

"We've kept this picture for so long;
I give it now to you."
Their moist eyes showed what they felt:
The years seemed gone, like dew.

"I wish we had a picture
"Of all our boys as well.
"I guess it's different with your first. . ."
Her wistful comments fell.

Later on at home that night
I wept to realize
That truly, one word: faithful,
Has characterized their lives.

I pictured them each night in prayer
On knees beside their bed
So all their children, one by one,
Could by our God be led.

The picture shows a life so small;
Yet now I'm fifty-two.
That tiny person who was me,
Would love their Jesus, too.

And now we've pledged, my spouse and I,
To also faithful be;
To bless and lift our children up
Each night before we sleep.

A better picture cannot be
Than of parents who will pray,
Faithful to the very end,
That God would bless and save.

Alissa's Day

When I go to bed at night,
I fold my hands to pray,
"Thank-you, Jesus, for my world;
I've had a happy day!"

My grandma pushed me on the swing,
Played in the sandbox, too.
I ran around on legs so strong,
And I say, "God, thank-you!"

We blew some bubbles on the deck
And walked around the flowers.
I picked up sticks and played in dirt;
My watering can made showers.

In the house we had a snack,
A cookie and a pear.
I washed it down with sips of milk,
Then went to play downstairs.

I liked to hold the small toy dog,
And Grandma sang fun songs
With me riding in the stroller,
As she pushed me on and on.

After lunch I had my nap,
Watched videos, a few:
Veggie Tales, Pooh Bear and Spot.
I squished some Playdough, too.

After work, my mommy came
To take me home; and then
The next day mommy goes to work,
We'll do it all again.

And then I go to bed at night,
Fold little hands and pray:
"Thank-you, Jesus, for my world;
I've had a happy day!"

Women

There are women of power
And women of greed,
Women of influence
And desperate need.

There are women of jealousy,
Women of pride,
Women of worry,
Withering inside.

There are women of godliness,
Prayer and good deeds,
Women of faithfulness—
God's ways they heed.

There are women of honor,
And if you're like me,
A Spirit-led woman
You desire to be.

Diary of a Mad Housewife

Clean the house, scrub the floor,
Wipe those smudges off the door.
Do the laundry, take out trash,
Clean the sink, then make a dash
To the grocery store, and then
Come back home and call a friend.

"My life's so busy," you complain;
"My husband really is a pain!
My kids—they drive me up a wall—
I just don't like my life at all!
It's time for me; where's my career?
I want fulfillment; can't you hear?

My life's a mess. What did you say?
I gotta run, I can't delay.
I'll miss that sale at T. J. Maxx
If I don't hurry up and act!
Run, run, run, that's all I do!
I wonder where I put my shoes . . ."

Teen Years

Gone are the years of total authority
As we give him space to make
More of his own choices.
This seems so strange, so painful,
So different.
I, who am used to being in control
Of my son's activities,
His hair style and his clothes.

I see the pain in his eyes
As he tries
To fit in in with his peers.
I hear wavering in a voice
Unsure of itself.
Will the values I taught him
Hold fast in his heart?
I feel anger as the girls
Call him on the phone
Night and day,
Keeping him from his studies and chores.

I complain about his irresponsibility,
His irritating manners.
I feel so unsure of myself;
I want to be his friend
And at the same time authoritarian.
These are rough, unchartered waters for me.
Sometimes, I feel he puts a foot
On me and flattens me,
Taking his own course,
Doing as he wills.
And I feel hurt and angry.

Can I trust him?
I have taught him the right,
But will he do the right and resist
The pressure to conform
To what surrounds him?
My boy, growing into manhood
Almost against my will—
And yet, I don't mean that.
I want him to be all
He can be: to excel,
Be strong, manly,
Of noble character,
Love and good deeds.

A little lady down the street
Captured his attention.
All those girl calls stopped
One by one,
And I was so glad
He found a good, Christian girl.

Sometimes he makes me laugh so hard
My sides ache,
And we share many close moments,
Free to discuss most anything.

Into Freedom

I hate the fact
That I feel the need
To be reassured
About my child's spiritual health.

I play fears
From the soundtrack of my mind,
Painting images there
That would like to "drive me bananas"
With wondering. Speculation. What if?
Would he really do that?
No, he couldn't possibly!
But then again, maybe he would?
Distrust. Uncertainty.
Needing reassurance.
How small of me.
Why do I struggle so?

Am I the only mother
Who feels like this?
If I am caught off-guard,
I can be driven to misery for hours
With mental anguish
Until I wake up and realize:
It's happened to me—again!
Then I repent, and speak God's word
Over my child,
Speaking what I expect
God to do in his life.
Speaking my faith.

I put that image
On the screen of my mind,
And I am at peace.

Whatever things I desire
When I pray,
I believe I receive them
When I pray,
And I shall have them
Sooner or later.
Keep the image up.
Give the Holy Ghost
Something to work with.
"Be not weary while doing good,
For in due season I shall reap
If I do not lose heart."[8]
Then I find peace.

Has any other mother
Felt like plastering the walls
Of "home sweet home"
With Scripture verses
To make sure her child
Will hear God shout at him?
Later, I am filled with shame
At such compulsion.

I must remember:
God brought me into
A love relationship with Himself,
And he can do the same
With my children.
He cares about them

---

[8] Galatians 6:9 (My paraphrase of NKJ)

Even more than I do.
Now, that's something
I'm prone to forget.
I've been so used to being
Responsible.

How well I remember
Feeling responsible for everything
In years past!
Uptight and feeling responsible
For myself, for others,
Not even trusting
My own husband sometimes.
Feeling driven to know everything
And fix everything.
Afraid to even trust God
With the life He gave me.
Afraid to let go the puny rope
Of my self-effort
That is about to snap.

If I fear what I can't see,
I can also have faith
For what I can't see.
And when I let go,
I fall upon the Word,
Finding sure and trustworthy promises
Abounding there—
A rich feast for my tormented soul.

I need to constantly
Accept my limitations
And entrust my anxieties to God,

Casting all my care on Him,
For He cares for me.
Easier said than done.
But do it, I will.
By God's help, I will!

Watch and Pray

Mark thirteen, twenty-six to thirty-seven,
Tells is Christ will come from heaven.
Be alert! Stay on guard!
We are given solemn charge.
Stay awake, do not sleep!
Jesus tells us watch to keep.

In Mark fourteen, thirty-eight,
Temptation's lurking at our gate.
Jesus says to watch and pray;
Escape is made for us that way.
With spirit eager, body weak,
We need our God; His help we seek.

Take care your hearts are not weighed down
With things of dissipation,
Anxiety and drunkenness,
Intemperance, diversion,
Lust for power, lust for greed,
Thinking we have all we need—
Repent!
What makes you sleep?
What anesthesia?
Lulled to sleep
With things that please you.
Cares of life, with same effect,
Steal your faith—you don't suspect.

Our Jesus will come
Like a thief in the night
To those of the dark,
Who aren't of the light.

Let's not be like others
Who lie, fast asleep;
But let's be alert,
Prayerful vigil to keep.

Be strong in the Lord,
The power of His might.
Put God's armor on,
Refuse to take flight.

With salvation's helmet,
Belt of truth on,
Breastplate of righteousness,
The Spirit's sword don.

With shield of faith raised,
Feet walking in peace,
Pray in the Spirit;
Let joy never cease.

Be alert and keep praying
For all of the saints.
May God give us boldness,
His Word to proclaim.

Stand firm in our struggle
Against evil powers,
Spirits of wickedness
That come in dark hours.

For God did appoint us
To not suffer wrath,
But to receive salvation
Through our Lord Jesus Christ.

(Sermon in a poem based on Mark 13:26 – 37; Luke 21:34 – 36; I
Thessalonians 5:1 – 11; Ephesians 6:10 – 18)

My People

We long to see God's power;
We ask His aid to lend.
We honor Him with mouth and lips,
But don't think to repent.

We point the finger at our nation—
How rotten to the core!
Yet fail to have a humble heart
So God could show us more.

Pontificate and legislate—
We will struggle on
Seeking change in our own way.
Repentance we must learn.

God promised healing for our land
If we ourselves repent.
Repentance is a gift from God;
Forgiveness, heaven-sent.

Are we willing, then, to leave them,
Sins that bar the door
To prisons of our own making,
And kneel in tears before the Lord?

Repent of prideful attitudes
And wanting praise of man,
Of unkind words and gossip;
We must call sin "a sin."

Repent of wanting to control,
To change the hearts of others,
Of sinful thoughts and actions
Against our sisters and our brothers.

Let freedom ring, let healing come!
Let hearts be white as snow!
Let praise arise, now sanctified,
As God His power shows.

(Sermon in a poem based on Isaiah 29:13; Isaiah 30: 1 – 3; 2 Chronicles 7:14; James 5:26)

A Soul Set Free

I was floating on life's sea
As all of us must do.
I got involved and weighted down
With things that made me blue.

The worldly things I'd anchored to
Just couldn't bear the strain
Of doubts and fears, of sins and tears.
I searched for help in vain.

I slowly settled in the mire;
My sins had weighed me down.
And when I'd dare to think of God,
I thought He wore a frown.

One day the Spirit slowly stirred
Down through the water deep
And raised my soul into the light
To find that God loved me!

I never thought that God up there
Would care so much for me,
That He would take His only Son
And hang Him on a tree!

Oh, precious Jesus, Savior mine,
My tongue cannot express
My love and gratitude to you.
You brought me happiness!

Jesus Cried with Me

We swabbed his mouth and kissed his head.
We children stayed around his bed;
Helped Daddy hug our mama's neck
As Mama kissed her love and wept.
And Jesus cried with me.

When Daddy couldn't eat or drink,
Or even make his eyes to blink,
We stroked his limbs, massaged his feet;
Sang songs that to him were so sweet.
And Jesus cried with me.

In tears we bathed his heated brow
Until he needed it no more.
When breath grew shallow, heartbeat faint,
God was there and saw His saint.
And Jesus cried with me.

Remembered words, remembered deeds,
When Daddy tended to our needs.
We told him "thanks" for all he'd done,
Then released him to go home.
And Jesus cried with me.

True Love

Jesus walks the road of life with me.
He meets me where I am
And takes my hand in His.
He speaks no words,
But the tears in His eyes
As He looks into mine
Speak volumes.

He stands still, with me, waiting.
A Man of sorrows
And acquainted with grief,
He respects the loss I feel
And offers His friendship in silence.

I am deeply moved as I see the Man,
Creator and God-Teacher,
Yet lowly Nazarene,
Coming to where I am
To walk the road of life with me.
I have so many questions;
His eyes are love,
And my heart is knit to His.

Peace and Plenty

Father, You are good and kind;
You bring healing to my mind.
With tender, watchful, loving care,
You thwart the lies of Satan there.

When I am down and in distress,
You lift my soul to happiness.
When fears assail, and doubts prevail,
The prayer of faith will never fail.

You bless my head with oil sweet;
I love Your goodness to repeat.
You're the Shepherd of my soul;
You know how to make me whole.

Though I walk through valleys deep,
I know that You my soul will keep.
A table You've prepared for me;
Your love and mercy I shall see.

(Based on Psalm 23)

My Man

He sticks with me through thick and thin;
He's calm, reserved and steady.
My husband's love protects and heals
When I'm distressed already.

A man of God with tender heart,
A man of faith is he.
A man of honesty and truth—
It's plain for all to see.

A man of many talents, too,
Soft-spoken and a fixer.
Reliable, advising, kind,
These words describe his picture.

A handyman, a boss at work;
He's steady as she blows.
A man respected and sought out
By everyone he knows!

The Teacher

Tender plant that sprang from seed
Watched with special care
By him who sees the young one's need,
And renders to him there

The love and nourishment to grow,
To flourish and to stand;
Through rains that come and winds that blow,
He lends a steady hand.

He may seem small and little-known,
This one who sees the need.
But by and by there will be shown
Good fruit for all to see.

Perfect Love

God put a robe of love on our sinful souls;
It makes us righteous in His holy eyes.
All praise to God for His great love and power!
All praise to Him because He makes us whole.

Chorus:
How we thank You, Lord, for Your perfect love;
Thanks for giving us this gift from above.
Hallelujah! Let's all cry aloud—
Great is Jehovah! Amen! Praise the Lord!

His overflowing love then had been satisfied
When to the cross He led His only Son to die.
And in His suffering, Jesus cried, "Forgive!"
Christ knew a sinner's death, so we might live.

We are now gifts to God above, forevermore!
We are delightful to His eyes, and in His plan.
Forever let us honor, praise and glorify
The God who stooped to help this sinful race called man.

Deliverance

Holy Spirit, Laser Light,
Pierce his heart with all Your might!
Walls will crumble to the ground
As fervent prayer will now abound.

Darkness flees as light is shined
Into the darkness of his mind.
Let fear of God be put in place
That he'll experience changing grace.

Let reverence for Your word be held
In high esteem so lies are felled!
He'll speak Your word as truth is sown;
Demonic captor shall be gone!

To Jesus

Thanks for coming
To the earth,
Thank You for
Your lowly birth.
Thanks for giving
Us Your worth;
Thanks for gracing
Home and hearth.

Thanks for love
And power shown
To those in need,
Who feel alone.
Thanks for truth
And favor, too.
May we bless
In all we do.

Snow

Ceased the hustle and the bustle
Of life's everyday events,
Now replaced with peace and quiet
By snow that's heaven-sent.

Hushed the sound of city's clamor,
Stilled the noisy motor throng
By thick blanket of white wonder.
We'll be snowed in all day long!

Time to break out that new puzzle,
Or perhaps read my new book,
Curl up with a cup of cocoa,
Or just stand right here and look.

Who can measure all the treasure
Found in show so clean and bright,[9]
Secrets hidden in the darkness
Only God can bring to light?

---

[9] Based on Job 38:22

Talkin' Turkey

I'm thankful for the turkey,
Potatoes, gravy, stuffing.
I'm thankful for the oyster stew.
But if thankfulness means stuffin'
My belly 'til I'm puffin',
I'd rather do without, thank you!

Mama's House

Apple pies, pumpkin pies,
Turkey, stuffing, more;
Smells so warm and comforting
Greet me at the door.

Mama's arms are open wide,
The table's all prepared.
Daddy comes with greeting, too;
Smiles and hugs are shared.

Our family forms a circle,
Hold hands, and then we sing
"I Thank the Lord My Maker,"
Who gives us everything.

Those special days at Mama's house
Are long remembered still.
Dad's missing from our circle now—
A space that none can fill.

Nature's Cue

Rustling leaves beneath the feet
Of squirrels that scamper to the beat
Of urgent winter storage plans,
Blow about by wind's command.

Withered too the flower's head,
Naked trees with leaves now shed;
Indian Summer skies of blue,
Geese that follow nature's cue—

These all signal summer's end;
Winter's just around the bend
When nature sleeps in white array
To burst awake on distant day.

Punctuation of Life

Exclamation points are wow!
Fun times make good glue.
Stop the run-on sentence now;
Put a period, too.

Semi-colon, hyphen, dash—
Parentheses and comma,
Apostrophes and question marks
Will add a punch of drama.

Brackets and quotation marks
Make merry out of life;
The colon and ellipsis too
Will help to sound the fife.

So, on the treadmill of the same,
Don't forget to party
As you step from day to day;
Please live hale and hearty!

Family Ties

Making time, taking time,
Busy moms and dads
Reap rewards in children's eyes
For all their years to come.

A time to read, a time to play
Will gladden children's hearts.
A smile, a wink, a funny shared,
Will surely make their day.

Feeling loved and understood
Builds trust in tender minds.
Expressing needs and giving heed
Will save from deepest wound.

Making time, taking time,
Busy moms and dad
Reap rewards in children's eyes
For all their years to come.

The Girl from Paradise

"I don't work outside the home,"
I answered in reply
To one who asked me if I worked.
Her eyes reflected, "Why?"

I turned to go, ashamed to speak
With one so worldly-wise.
What could I have in common with
A gal from paradise?

With lowered eyes, I felt a blush
Creep up across my cheek.
Dishes, laundry, packing lunch,
Were memories of my week.

Little kids with grimy face,
And jelly on the door,
Cleaning, cooking, changing sheets—
My life held no allure.

In my car and headed home,
As hot tears filled my eyes,
God whispered to my fragile soul
"You're my girl from Paradise!"

Talk Less, Pray More

When our pleasant expectations
Turn to many irritations,
When anger turns to conflagration—
Talk less, pray more!

When that someone really hurts you,
When the bills are such an issue,
When your life just needs a breakthrough—
Talk less, pray more!

When the elephants and donkeys
Make you scratch your head like monkeys,
'Till you're feelin' rather funky—
Talk less, pray more!

What Is Love?

Love is the glue
That keeps friendship from crumbling.
Love is the arm
That keeps you from stumbling.

Love is the look
That says, "It's okay,"
When you've behaved badly,
Or gone your own way.

Love is the joy
When truth wins the day;
Iniquities pardoned,
Not put on display.

Love is no joke;
It's sincere and kind,
Not rude or proud,
But peace for the mind.

Yes, love never fails,
And our God is love.
Our cues are from Him
On the wings of a Dove.

(Based on I Corinthians 13:4 – 8)

Mama's Hands

Her skin is thin and blood veins show;
Wrinkles you will see.
Though numb and pained and worn from work,
Their touch is Mama's love for me.

Sisters

Though not by birth,
We share a bond
As good as any sister.
Except for God
Who guides our paths,
I surely would have missed her.

My heart feels free
When I'm with her;
She understands my heart.
The thoughts we share,
Those times of prayer,
Bring a refreshing start.

Who can find
A faithful friend
Who sticks through thick and thin?
I'm blessed indeed
That I have found
A heart that is my twin.

Against All Hope

Frigid temperatures
Had chilled her to the bone
By a winter that raged against her marriage
As storm after storm
Had swept over her raw emotions
That threatened to buckle
Under the crushing weight
Of remembered abuse.

Would the long winter never end?
Would soft, warm breezes
Ever blow for her again?
Would Sonlight
Break through heavy clouds
And stop the chilling rain?

Everywhere in nature,
A long, cold winter
Had given way
To resurrection life.
The bright, floral colors of spring
Mocked her inner pain.
Creeping Phlox indeed!
Would to God
Their beauty
Could creep into her heart.
Tulips opened wide their cups
To embrace the sun.
How could she ever
Open her heart
To trust again?

In the panorama
Of the great outdoors,
The delicate lace of mint-green leaves
Bobbed in the breeze.
Dainty buds of magenta and white,
As well as yellow daffodils,
Nodded agreement
That spring had come.

A chill swept across her skin.
Could spring ever come
To her heart again?
She hugged herself
And went inside
To pray and wait.

(Written when a woman shared the pain in her marriage with me)

Salt

Though it cost me friend or favor,
From God's truth I'll never waver.
How can others see the Savior
If the salt has lost its flavor?

(Based on Matthew 5:13)

Closet Guest

You hang around without a sound,
Protect from stormy blast.
You laugh at cold, and I've been told
You'll work when fall has passed.

I see you there, and I don't care
That you're not needed yet!
Too soon I'll dote on you, my coat;
Your work I can't forget.

To Live in Freedom

I'm thankful that I have a home,
A quiet place to call my own—
Not homeless, wandering around.
I count my blessings; they abound!

Others live in constant fear
Of bombs and missiles coming near.
Children wail, and parents cry.
Heaps of rubble meet the eye.

William hides beneath his bed,
At angry words his father said
To his mom; it brought such fright
He cringed at sounds in dead of night.

Hopeless hoarder wades through trash;
In her house, there's just a path.
Angry, broken, in despair,
Life weighs too much to even care.

Wickedness pulls Christians down;
There's much trouble all around.
Racial hatred, great offense—
None of it makes any sense.

I'm thankful for our country dear
In spite of all the wrong that's here.
To live in freedom—oh how blessed!
May families live in godliness.

Love Acts

Love
Came to earth as a baby,
Grew up an obedient boy,
Worked as a carpenter,
Overcame all temptation,
Operated as a man in the power of the Holy Spirit,
Healed the sick,
Touched and cleansed the leper,
Cast out devils,
Raised the dead,
Opened deaf ears,
Blessed the children,
Fed thousands on a boy's lunch,
Gave scathing rebuke
To conniving, religious mindsets,
Made whips of cords,
Drove out the moneychangers,
Forgave the sinner,
Said, "Go, and sin no more."[10]

Love
Called the king a fox,
Walked on water,
Stilled the storm,
Paid His taxes,
Angered the Pharisees,
Taught heaven's truth,
Delegated authority,
Included Judas,
Prayed for us,

---

[10] John 8:11

Suffered at the hands of people,
Gave up His life for us on a painful cross,
Was buried in a tomb,
Rose in victory over death on the third day,
Provided salvation for all,
Triumphed over Satan's works,
Ascended into heaven,
Sent the Holy Spirit,
Offered forgiveness to all,
Is coming to earth again!

Love lives forever!

Window Pain

Baby blue or green or brown,
Eyes say much without a sound.
He sees into your window pain,
Emotions that still bring the rain.

He sees the pain that no one hears—
Discomfort, shame, uncertainties.
Let Him break your window pain
And make those dull eyes clear again.

He'll wash them gently with His love,
Anoint them with His gentle Dove.
He'll wipe your eyes and kiss your face,
So you can see amazing grace.

Song of Victory

Lift up the hands that hang down,
Let your mouth sing His praise!
Shake off the things that weigh down,
Speak Jesus' mighty name!

Let praise now arise!
Lift your voice to the skies!
Choose faith over fear;
His word, your heart will cheer.

Chorus:
Jesus, worthy, worthy Lamb!
Jesus, You're the great I Am!
Jesus, worthy, worthy Lamb!
Jesus—You are still the same!

Believe

Some children sniff at prophecy,
And roll their eyes at tongues;
Say miracles are passed away—
That healing's come and gone.

Believers, hear your Father;
Believe His holy Son!
Believe His Word and you will see
His gifts are going strong!

Growing

Resting on the bosom of Jesus,
Enjoying all His tender care,
Show me how to draw from you, Savior,
The peace and help that I see there.

Problems come that I can't handle,
'Til I come and tell You all.
Then you put me on a road called Victory!
You surely hear me when I call.

Read the Word with care and study;
Make your heart a soil fine,
That the truth may take root deeply,
And produce true faith that shines.

Lean your entire being on Jesus,
Spirit, body, soul, and mind.
Depth in prayer with God will free you
To leave all old ways behind.

Victory Armor

I do not ask for visions fair
Of Jesus Christ in splendor there.
Just let me sit down at His feet,
And learn of His triumphant sweep
Of victory over Satan's sting
When Christ to earth God's love did bring.

Oh hallelujah, Savior mine!
Your sovereign power alone shall shine.
The gates of hell You did defeat
To give Your child Your victory sweet.
Teach me how to use the sword,
To thrust doubt through with God's true word.

Salvation's helmet on my head,
His oil of gladness on me shed—
I wear the robe of righteousness;
All I can do is now confess
That Jesus Christ is King of kings,
And Lord of any earthly thing.

My feet must wear the shoes of peace
To take firm stand, and never cease
To be on guard. The truth I wear
And bind it tight, to lose it ne'er.
The lifted shield of faith shall quench
All fiery darts that Satan sends.

So, praise the Lord, O child of God!
You walk not where but He has trod.
You are in Christ and He in you,
And Jesus is your armor true.
So, put on Christ by your free well,
And hear Him whisper, "Peace! Be still!"[11]

(Based on Ephesians 6:10 – 18)

---

[11] Mark 4:39

Be Still

Be still and know that He is God.

Do not worry, do not fret.
Those things that you imagine
Have not happened yet.
Why borrow trouble? Why feel dismayed?
Fix your thoughts on good things—
God will come to your aid.

Be still and know that He is God.

Don't run here, don't run there,
Fighting just to beat the air.
Take your stand, as Jesus said.
You wear a crown upon your head.
Watch Him work; what do you see?
Jesus gives the victory!

Sweet Spring

I close the door and lock the latch
To walk the walk four blocks and back.

I breathe in deep, and smell the sweet;
The scent and sight of flowers meet.

Yellow, purple, pink and white
Fill my senses with delight.

Fingertips of soft mint green
Grace the trees in lovely scene.

Bird songs fill my ear with sound;
Squirrels cavort along the ground.

Lawns are manicured with care;
My face is kissed by sun-warmed air.

Winter's chill and blahs give way
To warbles, tweets, and sun-filled day!

The Sluggard

Go to the ant now, O sluggard;
Consider her ways and be wise.
Turn off the telly, stretch out the belly;
Open the lids of your eyes.

How long will you lie there, O sluggard?
When will you rise from your sleep?
Just one more snooze and the folding of hands
Will put you in debt way too deep.

I went past the field of the sluggard,
Past the vineyard of him who was slack.
Thorns had grown through his garden,
The ground and the wall were a wreck.

I took to heart ways of the sluggard.
A lesson was learned, and I knew
A little more sleep and the folding of hands
Will keep me from things I should do.

(Based on Proverbs 6:10; Proverbs 24:30 – 34)

Humility

Pride goes before destruction,
Haughty spirit precedes a fall.
Before honor comes humility—
We'll do well to recall.

With wisdom comes humility:
A treasure from the heart.
Acknowledge God in all my ways,
And know I'm not that smart!

Think not more highly than you ought,
Exalt yourself no more.
Avoid disgrace, receive His ways,
And enter lowly door.

(Based on Proverbs 15:33, Proverbs 16:18, Proverbs 13:10, Proverbs 29:23, Proverbs 11:2, Psalm 25:9, James 4:6, and Matthew 23:12)

Juggling

We juggle the news,
We juggle our fears.
We juggle our friends,
We juggle our tears.

We juggle our problems,
We juggle our kids.
We juggle our mates,
We juggle and skid.

Life gets in a hurry;
We don't stop to say,
"What am I doing
Juggling that 'J'?"

Virtuous Woman

She may not wear high fashion,
Or go about with airs.
She may not have the latest "do,"
Or know about "The Bears."

But clothed with strength and dignity,
She laughs at days to come.
She knows it snows, and has no fear
As she protects her home.

Her children rise and call her blessed,
And husband sings her praise.
She does him good and never harm,
The full length of his days.

He lacks no confidence in her,
She works with eager hands.
Her arms are strong for every task;
In business, takes her stand.

Her heart is for the needy,
Instruction's on her tongue.
Charm deceives and beauty leaves,
But love goes on and on.

(Based on Proverbs 31:10 – 31)

The Gift of Laughter

Laughter is the zest of life,
The zip that springs your step.
The trigger for your body's health,
The thing that fuels your pep.

It's free, it's fun, it eases pain,
Improves your mood and stress;
Protects the heart, increases strength,
And makes you feel so blessed.

Infectious laughter is a gift;
We all need lots of fun.
Laughter lifts, delights and heals,
And makes our hearts feel warm.

Yesterdays

Don't go playing in the street!
Wash your hands and wipe your feet.
Eat your veggies, clean your plate.
Let me kiss that little face.
Sometimes I miss my yesterdays.

The kids at play in dusky light,
Chasing, catching fireflies.
Teeth are brushed, prayers are said;
Then I tuck them into bed.
Sometimes I miss my yesterdays.

To the bus stop—here's your lunch!
Please tell me your homework's done.
Before you walk out of sight,
You turn around and wave "Goodbye."
Sometimes I miss my yesterdays.

Rides to church, and "zip to keep,"
Clyde the goat, jokes from back seat,
Ice cream on the long drive home,
Laughing much and having fun.
Sometimes I miss my yesterdays.

Short Stories

House of Cards

Monique felt sick at heart. Once again, Jake had come home drunk and high; she hoped he'd just go upstairs and sleep it off. She was tired of making excuses for her husband, hiding his addictions from their son Gib, and phoning in sick for Jake at his work. Tired of cleaning up his messes. Gib was fast losing respect for his dad, and no wonder. She had lost respect for Jake as well. The ache in her heart found its way to her head, and she searched in a kitchen cabinet for an Advil to kill the pain. If only life's messes could be fixed by a pill. . . Her thoughts trailed away.

She wished she'd been more discerning before marrying Jake, wished she'd heeded her mother's and grandmother's warnings, wished they had been married in a church . . . She washed down the pill with a glass of water, and then sat down at the kitchen table, wondering if maybe she should eat a soda cracker or two with the Advil. Putting her head in her hands, an old saying she'd heard somewhere came to mind: "If wishes were horses, beggars would ride."

Hot tears threatened to erupt as her mind replayed her mother's words: "You've made your bed—now sleep in it!" The memory still stung. For the first time in a long time, she regretted she'd chosen to distance herself from her family. She felt so alone. Hadn't spoken to her mother or grandmother in years. Somehow, it just seemed easier to go on living without the entanglements of a meddling family and difficult relationships. What was it her grandmother had said? Her head throbbed as she remembered: "Build your house on Jesus, the Rock, Monique; a house built on the sand is no better than a house of cards. The storms of life will destroy it."

Now she was living in that proverbial house of cards: a house that would surely crumble and be scattered to the wind if that storm grew any stronger. She toyed with the idea of leaving Jake. But if she did, what would happen to Gib? How would she make a home for the two of them? She was already working long hours at a job that drained her. And what would happen to Jake? What would it do to him? Would he spiral out of control even worse than he did now if she left him or told him to get out? Where would he go if she did ask him to leave? Was there hope of getting a new start, a solid foundation, a house built on the Rock, like her grandmother said? Were there any second chances? The questions swirled through her head like the spiral arm in a slushy machine at a fast food restaurant.

Jake. She knew he hadn't had an easy life. He'd been in and out of foster homes since he was five years old, didn't know who his father was, and was abandoned by his mother on a street corner in New York City. "Wait here," she had told him; "I'm going inside the bakery to get us a treat. Now you be good and stay here till I come. I'll be right back." But she never came back. A policeman had found him crying, and Jake was placed into foster care until he was eighteen. She knew his painful scars of betrayal went deep.

She had been so sure that once they were married, her love for him would be enough to change him and make him happy. Instead, everything she tried to do to change him made him moody and irritable. So far, he'd never physically hit her, but in anger he'd grabbed her and pinned her to the wall. There'd been many verbal battles. He went out nights more and more and stayed away longer and longer. The relentless question she dreaded pressed itself into her mind: is he seeing someone else? Where did he go at night, and why did he stay away so long? Her knight in shining armor was badly tarnished. Why couldn't she polish him?

Monique longed for peace. She remembered how happy she'd been during those early days of their marriage, how they did things together, how much they were in love. Feelings of loneliness constricted her throat as she bit back the tears. After all, she had made her own bed and had to lie in it, just like Mom had said. Mom. Where could she turn to for help? She was sure a phone call to her mother would be unwelcome and deeply humiliating. Her mother's words echoed in her heart: "If you leave this house, girl, don't you ever come back to me for help! Her mom's final words still had its effect, and she'd kept her distance—physically and emotionally.

In desperation, she thought of the Bible she had sometimes read as a teenager. She tried to remember where it was as her conscience pricked her. *Probably still packed away in the moving boxes from six months ago,* she thought to herself. It seemed they were always moving from place to place since the day they got married.

Monique looked at the dishes piled in the sink that couldn't be put into the dishwasher until she unloaded the clean ones and put them away. The floor needed cleaning where Jake had tracked in mud when he came home. She tried to focus her thoughts. *What to do first? That was the question. Priorities. Yes, that was it. Set some priorities. Get moving—do something. Don't just sit here and brood.*

She got to her feet just as Gib came bounding down the stairs and snarled, "I'm going out. Don't bother to wait up for me." Her question of "Where are you going?" was lost to the air as her teenage son disappeared out the front door, slamming it hard behind him.

Stunned by his rude behavior and tone of voice, Monique covered her face with her hands and let herself have an old-fashioned cry. As she sobbed, she heard herself say, "Oh God, oh God, please help me. Help my family." She hadn't prayed in years. Where was that Bible? A feeling of hope began to invade her mind.

In the basement, Monique opened boxes and searched in earnest. *It must be here somewhere.* An hour passed, and her arms and back ached. She found her grandmother's picture in a box with some clothes from ten years ago. *Why am I keeping those clothes anyway?* The thought irritated her. If she wouldn't have so much to unpack, she'd have found the Bible by now. People said she looked a lot like her grandmother. Monique wondered what she'd look like in a 50's hairstyle. *Maybe those people were right. . .*

Her hand found a book; quickly she flung aside an old bathrobe and bedroom slippers and pulled it out of hiding. It was the novel, *Gone with the Wind.* Shucks. *And how appropriate*, she thought grimly. She'd have to keep looking. As she pawed through skirts and blouses, Monique's fingers closed around another book. She'd found her Bible! She hugged it to her chest, fled upstairs with it and her Grandmother's picture, leaving the basement in a mess.

Monique switched on the lamp by the overstuffed chair in the living room, sank down into the chair's welcome softness and opened her Bible. An envelope fell out. *What is this?* The envelope was still sealed, and as she turned it over, she saw her name on the front. Monique took the envelope to the kitchen, turned on the overhead row of bulkhead pot lights, found a paring knife, and quickly slit the long edge open. Leaning against the countertop and with shaking hands, she took out a letter dated August 20, 1994, addressed to her:

Dear Monique,

By the time you read this, I may already have passed on to the other side. But I want you to know that my prayers for you are still alive; they never die. I also want you to know that I love you very much.

I will admit I am distressed you've chosen to elope with Jake and are now married. I would have liked the chance to see you walk down the aisle of our church and know that you and Jake have a solid foundation for your marriage. However, that is not the way things worked out, so I want to put a few words on paper for you and pray the day will soon come when you will find this letter I tucked in your Bible.

My dear granddaughter, Jesus is the only solid foundation for a life or marriage. Even if you may seem to lose your way, call out to Jesus and talk to Him. Read the Bible and believe what it says to you. Find Matthew 7:24-27 and put the words of Jesus into practice in your life. God is not angry with you. Jesus paid for all our sins, including yours and mine. All have sinned; there is no one who is righteous without Jesus—no, not one person! He is waiting for you to come to Him and believe what He says. Find Romans 10: 9-10; read it, believe it, and do it.

I pray you and Jake will build your marriage on the solid Rock that is Jesus. My prayers always follow you.

God bless you always.

Your loving grandmother,

Violet

As Monique finished the letter, her eyes blurred with tears that fell in large drops onto her grandmother's handwriting.

She found a tissue and mopped the tears from her face and blew her nose. After she washed her hands, she unloaded and put away the clean dishes, then re-loaded the dishwasher, put a Cascade Complete tablet in the dispenser, closed the lid, selected the cycle and pushed the "start" button. Next, she wiped down the counters and sink with kitchen disinfectant.

After she swept the kitchen floor and damp-mopped it, she turned off the kitchen light, picked up the letter and returned to the comfort of the chair in the living room. Gib still wasn't home. *What if he's out there with bad company doing God only knows what?* The thought plagued her.

Monique opened her Bible to Matthew 7:24-27 and read that the house built on the rock didn't fall during the rain, floods, and strong winds that beat against it. The house stood firm on the rock. That's what she wanted—no—needed. She was tired and very afraid in this house of cards. She had to have peace and an anchor. She read the Scripture in Romans her grandmother mentioned and thought about it.

Finally, in an attitude of surrender, Monique slipped to her knees in front of the chair and prayed, "Jesus, please forgive me of all my sins and the mess in my life. I want to have this solid foundation I read about here in the Bible. I need peace. I take you as the Lord and Savior of my life, to have and to hold forever. Please, God, help Jake's and my marriage to get on the right track, and help Jake to give his life to you, too." Peace and a sense of relief came over her. As she knelt there, tears again washed her face. The feeling of being loved was so wonderful, she couldn't explain it.

The front door opened and Gib walked in. Monique stood up, wiped her face with another tissue, and looked at her son. "Gib, where have you been? I've been so worried about you!" Monique walked toward him.

He held up his hand in protest: "I don't want to talk about it. You and Dad always fight, and I can't take it anymore! You think I don't know when he comes home drunk? You think I don't know he's doing drugs? He's a bum and doesn't even care about me. Just cares about himself."

"Gib, don't say that! Your father does love you—in his own way. He just doesn't know how to show it very well." Monique's eyes filled with tears as she looked down at the floor. She wondered if Jake even cared about himself. *Jesus, what can I tell my son? Please help me.*

Gib headed toward the kitchen through the living room to fix himself a sandwich and saw a Bible lying on the chair and asked, "Is that a Bible, Mom? Why are you reading it?"

Monique smiled at him through her tears and eagerly showed him her grandmother's letter and told how she asked Jesus to take over her life. "We need Jesus in our home, Gib. Your father, you, and I each need Him as the foundation for our personal lives."

"I don't know, Mom," Gib said. "What would my friends think if I go soft, 'n' get religion and all? And fat chance of getting Dad convinced." Gib turned and went upstairs.

"Don't you want a sandwich? You must be hungry since you missed dinner."

There was no answer.

Monique knelt by the chair and stayed on her knees for a long time after Gib went to bed.

***

Jake heard Monique hum a tune as she ran the Swiffer duster under the television and across the top. She smiled at him as she dusted the coffee table. For the past month she'd been acting weird. He went to the kitchen, came back with a beer and settled in his favorite arm chair to watch a M. A. S. H. re-run.

"Would you like a sandwich and chips, Jake?" Monique straightened the magazines on the coffee table.

Jake felt startled. Why was she being so nice to him? What had gotten into his wife? "Yes, that would be good," he replied.

He couldn't put his finger on it, but he wondered why she didn't yell back at him anymore when he yelled at her. A sudden thought occurred to him: *maybe she's having an affair!* The thought jolted him. He didn't matter to her anymore. Yes, that must be it. She was secretly planning to leave him. Just like his mother had left him all alone when he was five years old. The thought left him cold inside. The cutting pain of that memory fueled every bit of the feelings of distrust, fear and hate that rose inside him. Maybe he'd go out tonight and get some drugs and forget all this—at least for a while. Anything to stop the pain, the self-loathing, the emptiness inside. But then there was the problem of paying for the drugs and alcohol he'd come to see as the answer. Things were getting tight. . . but he wouldn't think of that now. He downed the beer and went to the fridge for another.

Monique was in the kitchen putting lettuce, Swiss cheese and pickles on top of a ham and turkey on rye. His favorite. He watched her put it on a plate and cut it in half. He felt cut in half. His soul felt like those pickles: biting and sour.

Would he dare tell her how he was feeling, what he was thinking? Deep down inside a part of him wanted to open up to her, but if she was planning to leave him, he had to defend himself. Watch his step. This was no time to go soft. What would it be like to have a happy family? To love and be loved without fear of rejection? Where did he and Monique go wrong? He wished they could go back to those first months of married life when he'd felt so sure Monique could fill the hole in his heart. Then Gib had been born, and it seemed she didn't have time for him anymore. Always busy with the baby. He admitted it: he'd resented her.

As his wife handed him the plate with the sandwich and chips, he grunted in brief recognition of the favor she'd done him and settled into his favorite chair again. He bit into his sandwich and was astonished that Monique joined him in the living room to watch television. She'd always had something else to do in the house— leaving him alone with his beer and shows. Why did she now have time to sit with him and watch a show she didn't especially care for? Something was up. . .

***

As Monique joined Jake in the living room to watch M. A. S. H., she thought of Rachel across the street. Thank God for friends! A month had passed since that life-changing night she found her Bible in the basement. Rachel had brought her daughter over to sell Girl Scout cookies three weeks ago. It turned out she and Rachel became good friends, and they began to study the Bible together twice a week. Rachel taught her about the free grace of God that lets us live in freedom toward Him. Monique confided her troubles to Rachel, who in turn helped her see God's truth about love and marriage in the Bible. She remembered how Rachel prayed with her for Jake and Gib to also make Jesus the Master of their lives. How wonderful it would be to all stand on the same foundation together!

She especially was grateful for the words in the book of I Peter 3 that Rachel showed her. Monique had memorized them: "Wives, in the same way, be submissive to your husbands so that, if any of them do not believe the word, they may be won over without words by the behavior of their wives, when they see the purity and reverence of your lives. Your beauty should not come from outward adornment, such as braided hair and the wearing of gold jewelry and fine clothes. Instead, it should be that of your inner self, the unfading beauty of a gentle and quiet spirit, which is of great worth in God's sight. For this is the way holy women of the past who put their hope in God used to make themselves beautiful. They were submissive to their own husbands, like Sarah, who obeyed Abraham and called him her master. You are her daughters if you do what is right and do not give way to fear."

Fear. Afraid if she didn't yell at Jake and stand up for herself, he'd walk all over her, take advantage of her. Could she trust God to take care of her if she stepped out in faith and obeyed God's word? Did that mean she couldn't have a mind of her own? Wasn't allowed to say what she thought and how she felt about something? When was the time to speak up and when was the time to be quiet?

You can speak up without yelling, Monique. You have a right to say how you feel and what you think, to speak the truth in love. Wow, did God just speak into her heart? She was amazed by the peace that came over her. Rachel had told her the Holy Spirit would speak to her and give her wisdom. And He really did! God could handle her problems; change Jake and Gib. Rachel said so, and she believed it. Yelling and scolding, blaming and shaming hadn't worked. Those things only drove her and Jake further apart.

Rachel told her that when a man is shown respect, he feels honored, which translates into feeling loved. She also learned that a guy loves to have his girl sit with him and just "hang out" without conversation. That was an eye-opener, and something she could do. With all that was in her, she was committed to making her marriage work, to ask God for help, and to give her wisdom. But a question plagued her: how could she respect Jake when he continued his current lifestyle? What did "showing respect" mean? She would talk some more to Rachel about that scripture about being quiet and submissive. One thing she felt certain of: God had the answer, and she would find it, somehow.

Monique's thoughts were silent prayers as she leaned her head against the back of her cushioned chair and watched Alan Alda, Wayne Rodgers, and Loretta Swit in action.

***

The television program was done. Jake looked over at Monique and studied her for a moment, trying to gather courage to say something. Monique gave him a smile.

"Why are you being nice to me?" There. He'd said it. Better to know the truth and get it over with. He braced himself for the answer.

"Oh Jake, the most wonderful thing has happened to me."

Without waiting for her to explain, Jake blurted, "Are you in love with someone else, Monique? Are you having an affair?" Jake couldn't help himself. He had to know.

Monique's mouth flew open and her eyes registered shocked surprise. Now he felt ashamed he'd even asked the question.

"No way, Jake! She reached over to put a hand on his arm, but he pulled away.

"I'm not in love with anyone else and I'm not having an affair! Why would you think that?" Monique's lips began to tremble.

Jake looked away from her and stood up to get another beer from the fridge.

Monique felt tearful as she followed him into the kitchen. "The most wonderful thing I'm talking about is what happened to me about a month ago here in the living room.

"I feel so afraid and alone when you're drunk or high, Jake. Four weeks ago, I was feeling like that when you came home and yelled at Gib. I was desperate for help and didn't know what to do. That night I remembered my grandmother saying that a home without the foundation of Jesus is like living in a house of cards. I asked God to help me. Then I thought of my Bible I used to read in high school, and I found it in a box in the basement. When I opened my Bible, a letter fell out. Would you like to read it?"

When Jake didn't answer, she opened the cabinet door below the television, got her Bible, found the letter, and handed it to him. Monique waited and prayed in silence as he read. *What should I say to him, Jesus? Help me to say it in the right way. Help me to speak the truth in love. Please work in his heart to accept Your truth, too.*

As he finished the letter, Jake kept his head lowered. When he looked up, there were tears in his eyes. "If this is true, why didn't someone tell me about Jesus sooner? The foster parents I had told me to 'do this, don't do that, because the Bible says so', but nobody ever told me Jesus loved me or paid for my sins. I could never be good enough to please my foster parents. Seemed they were always upset with me."

Monique asked, "May I show you the Scripture I read when I asked Jesus to save me from my sins?"

Jake looked at her as she turned to Romans 10:9 – 10 and read it aloud. Jake, would you like to pray to receive Jesus for yourself?" Monique held her breath. Surely the Holy Spirit was at work in her husband.

"Yes, I would, Monique; yes, I would."

In a broken voice, Jake began to speak to God in a child-like way. "God, I've made a mess of my life; please clean me up and give me a new life. I surrender my life to You and I say You are my Lord too, like Monique here. Help me be a good husband and forgive all my sins. I didn't know you paid for all my sins. I thought I had to be good, so You'd love me. Thank You for paying for all my sins."

In her own heart, Monique was praising and thanking God. Rachel taught her that Scripture says God's kind of love never fails. This had to be the secret of winning a spouse over to the Lord, just like that fellow Peter in the Bible said. *I can't wait to tell Rachel! And I'll give Mom and my grandmother a call tomorrow!*

As they stood to their feet, a new husband and a new wife embraced each other. They had exchanged their house of cards for the new beginnings of a house built on the Rock, Christ Jesus.

Note: I contributed this piece for an anthology titled *Short Story Revival* in 2017, published by Northern Virginia Christian Writer's Fellowship, of which I am a member. Reprinted by permission of PW Publishing, a division of Portrait Writer, LLC. I own the rights to this work.

The Angel That "Flied"

"I remember all that happened as though it were yesterday." Debbie leaned forward, thick, ash-blond hair falling attractively around her face. Her large, warm, clear blue eyes filled with tears as she told me the story.

"That Friday, I dropped off my four-year-old son, Danny, and his cousin, Melanie at my mom's town house, drove out of the complex and across the divided highway to the parked school bus I would drive come September. The road looked wet from the shimmer of the intense August heat, and the 100° felt like at least 120°. As I cleaned and washed out the bus, I kicked off my shoes to let the water cool my feet. Then, as I bent down to clean under a seat, I heard a voice say, 'Hi, Mommy!'

"I wheeled around, shocked to see my baby, my Danny, standing on the bus steps! I said, 'Danny! What are you doing here? I told you to stay at Grandma's! Now you stay right here; I'm just about finished.'

"I turned my attention to stuffing the ditty bag (first-aid kit, fire extinguisher, etc.). Suddenly, I heard the screech of brakes, and when I straightened and looked out the window, I saw a black Chevy Blazer had hit my son, who was lying motionless in the road. I leaped from the bus, forgetting my bare feet, and dashed to Danny's motionless form.

"My mind was becoming hysterical. Suddenly I felt my spirit take control of my mind, like something coming out of here." Debbie paused to demonstrate by laying her hands across her abdomen. "It seemed I somehow became only an instrument God was using, and I was filled with an overwhelming peace I never experienced before or since. I acted out the instructions from the scripture in Mark 16:18, 'Lay hands on the sick and they shall recover.' So, I laid hands on Danny's head, then his neck, chest, stomach, legs, and feet. I prayed aloud, 'Lay hands on the sick, and they shall recover,' repeatedly. I experienced what Jesus said in the Bible, John 7:38: 'Whoever believes in Me, out of his belly shall flow rivers of living water.'

"By this time a crowd had gathered around me and Danny. One man who heard me pray thought I was in shock, pulled me away from my son, and told me to call my husband. Reluctantly, I obeyed. But first, I called a Christian sister and asked her to call others.

"When I got back to the scene, the ambulance had arrived, and Danny was in the back. I got in beside him. As we started for Commonwealth Hospital, I saw a huge bump on the side of his head. Again, I began to pray. Laying my hands on his head, I said, 'In the Name of Jesus, there will be no brain damage to this child!' I didn't care who heard me.

"The ambulance went to the hospital on a code blue, and a paramedic named John urged me to call Danny's name. I shouted, 'Danny, in the name of Jesus, talk to me! Talk to me!' All at once, my son began to cry. 'That sound is music to our ears, Mom,' John said. 'We've placed him in the best hands—those of the Great Physician. I'm with Fishnet Ministries, and all three of us running this ambulance are born-again Christians, ma'am.'

"At Commonwealth, the doctors were grave. The X-rays did not look good, so he was transferred to the trauma unit at Fairfax Hospital in Fairfax, Virginia.

"Upon our arrival there, a group of Christians had gathered to pray with us as Danny was rushed to the second floor and prepped for surgery. Within the walls of a private room, we knelt in a circle, holding hands. As we prayed, someone spoke in tongues by the power of the Holy Spirit and gave the interpretation. The message was this: 'There will be no knife taken to this child. Jesus is on the scene, and He is the same yesterday, today, and forever. The eyes of man will see a miracle, and miracles are for the unbelievers.'

"We finished praying and sat down to wait. In just a few minutes the door burst open, and a frantic nurse beckoned with urgency. 'Mr. and Mrs. Mosher, Dr. Seneca wants to see you immediately! The X-rays are starting to contradict themselves, and he doesn't know what to think!'

"My husband and I jumped to our feet, and the prayer partners thanked and praised God. As we entered the trauma unit, Dr. Seneca met us. He looked quite moved as he announced, 'Danny does not need surgery. He started functioning on his own, but we want to keep him here for observation.'

"We spent that night with Danny in intensive care, and the nurses were incredulous that our son survived. The next day, Saturday, Danny was moved to a regular room! And on Sunday, Dr. Seneca released Danny to go home, and called him a miracle child as he offered a teddy bear to my son.

"My husband, Victor, and I were concerned about possible mental trauma in our son, so that afternoon we questioned him at home. I said, 'Danny, do you realize what happened to you, honey?'

"My four-year-old thought awhile, then said, 'Umm, I 'member the big black car hitted me, and then I went to sleep.' I asked him if that's all he remembered. His forehead creased in deep thought, then all at once his face brightened. 'I 'member the angel that flied, Mommy.'

"I was transfixed and asked him what he meant by seeing an angel. He replied, 'Yes, Mommy, you know—the angel that flied in the ambulance. The angel took my hands and placed them around my neck, like this.' Danny placed his small hands behind his own neck to demonstrate. 'And he carried me.'

"I asked him where he was carried, where he went. My son said, 'The angel took me to Jesus, Mommy. The angel said Jesus told him to go down in the road and get the little boy that was hurt.'

"Stunned, I asked him again if he really saw Jesus. When he replied, 'Uh-huh,' I asked him what Jesus looked like. He thought hard and struggled for the right words. Finally, my four-year old Danny said matter-of-factly, "Mommy, Him looked like a big, bright, bright light bulb! There was lights all around!'

"I asked him if he talked to Jesus. He nodded and said, 'Uh-huh.' I prodded him further and wanted to know what Jesus said to him. Danny said, 'Jesus said He was gonna heal me!'

"My curiosity got the best of me, and I asked him if he saw me, or any people, on the road at the scene of the accident. Danny said, 'No, Mommy, but I 'member the man sitting by the road with his hands on his head.'

"All of us in the room were stunned by what was just revealed. The man who hit Danny had been sitting on the curb with his head in his hands, just as Danny described him.

"Well, the burns on his back healed miraculously without medical treatment, and by Tuesday morning his left collar bone and large bump on his head were down flat. The doctors were incredulous; they had truly seen a miracle!

"Today, as I sometimes hold my son's hands in mine, I thank God for His kind goodness. Although I had been a Christian for many years, that August of 1984 was the time I lost my fear of God and I realized how much He loved me. He was not 'up there' with a club just waiting for me to sin so He could 'get me.' He allowed me to keep all three of my sons, yet gave up the only One He had for me!"

As Debbie spoke these words, her eyes brimmed with tears that spilled down her face. "I have a very thankful heart for who God is, and I firmly believe that having an attitude of heart-felt gratitude and faith in God's word are vital keys to experiencing the miraculous intervention of God.

***

I wrote this after my interview with Debbie Mosher in 1996 and sold the story to *Guideposts.* It made the cover story of their 1997 May/June issue of *Angels on Earth* magazine. They interviewed Debbie and re-wrote the story to their own liking and changed the title to "Silent Words for a Frightened Mother."

Original manuscript is owned by me, and used by permission of *Angels on Earth* magazine, a division of *Guideposts* magazine.

Man of Honor

Joseph's hand caressed the finished kitchen table. His trained eye drank in the exotic beauty of the olive wood as his finger traced the dark and light swirls in the grain. He had sanded the surface and used polishing agents on the treasured piece, rubbing it to a sheen until it gleamed under his expert hand. He'd also made matching benches, and if he did say so himself, the set was a thing of beauty—a wonderful gift worthy of his betrothed.

He smiled to himself and felt a blush creep up his neck as he thought of the sturdy bed he'd also fashioned for them. He'd go to Mary tonight and invite her to see what he had made for their home. *Soon everything will be ready, and I'll bring her home as my wife!* The thought filled his heart with great joy and contentment.

Joseph reflected on his bride-to-be as he made his way to Mary's house after his evening meal. She'd returned home from a three-month vacation to her cousin Elizabeth in Judea, and the visit must have done her good. He couldn't quite put his finger on it, but she had a glow about her, and seemed—well, older somehow. He'd never considered her especially beautiful, but now, in the few times he'd seen her around town recently, she seemed radiant, and his eyes drank in her extraordinary loveliness. He was grateful that God would give him such a blessing, especially at his age. He'd always liked her quiet manner and the fact that she wasn't giggly like other girls. The arranged marriage would be a good one.

At Mary's house, Joseph knocked on the door, and she opened it. They smiled at one another as their eyes met and she invited him in, took his cloak, and hung it on a wall peg. "I came to invite you to see what I've made for our home," Joseph announced. "When would it suit you?"

"I love surprises," Mary enthused. "I will be free tomorrow at mid-morning, if that suits you. Come, stay awhile before you return home. May I offer you something to eat?"

"Oh, no, I already ate, but I thank you anyway," Joseph answered.

As he and Mary walked to a sitting area, he noticed her body seemed different; she must have put on a little weight or something. He tried not to stare at her abdomen, and he caught Mary's furtive glance in his direction. They sat down together on the bench; Mary folded her hands tightly in her lap and looked away from him.

"Have you been well?" Joseph asked. Suddenly the atmosphere seemed strained between them. "It's been a while since I've seen you," he added, hoping to relieve the tension.

"Yes, I'm quite well, Joseph." Mary turned to him with a timid smile. "But I have something to tell you." She put her hand to her throat and paused for a moment.

Joseph waited.

"You may have heard some gossip about me…" Mary began.

"The only gossip I heard was of a girl being pregnant out of wedlock—but certainly not about you, my dear one."

Mary looked at him, then lowered her eyes to her belly.

Joseph tensed inwardly. He couldn't, wouldn't believe it. Fear gripped his soul. He closed his eyes tightly, swallowed hard, and took a deep breath before he dared speak. "Mary," Joseph whispered, "What are you saying? Are you...?" He glanced down at Mary's hands folded in her lap and noticed the distinct curve of her abdomen.

"It's not what you think, Joseph," Mary interrupted quickly. She looked at him with pleading eyes. Her slender fingers pushed back a tendril of black hair that escaped from her head veil, then adjusted the sleeves of her light blue dress before she clasped her hands together again. "Let me explain. An angel of the Lord came to me some months ago and said I would give birth to the Son of God, Israel's Messiah—our Messiah! He said the Holy Spirit would come upon me, and that I would conceive the Holy Child! Is that not wonderful?

His mind refused her information, and reeled, as all previous joy drained from him. Could it be? The snippets of gossip he'd heard around town about a girl pregnant out of wedlock *had* been about Mary! *His Mary!* A sudden thought jolted him: had she played the harlot while she was away in Judea? Waves of shocked disbelief and dismay pierced his soul at the thought. He felt violated, like someone had dumped black tar on his beautiful furniture. Dishonored. Disrespected. He shook his head as though to clear it of unwanted thoughts. Surely it wasn't true. But there was no getting around it—he had to face facts. Panic ripped a jagged chasm across his mind as he imagined the betrayal, and forced himself to whisper, "Who's...the father?"

Joseph stood to his feet, and Mary looked up at him with pleading eyes, still and silent. He looked away from her, crossed his arms and clenched his jaw. Mary spoke quietly. "It is as I said before, Joseph. The Child is of the Holy Spirit, just like the angel said. The angel also told me that my cousin Elizabeth had conceived a child in her old age and was in her sixth month. So, I went to Judea to celebrate with her, and it was just as I was told. While I was there, she gave birth to a son they named John. She truly had a miracle!"

"Yes, I heard she had a son in her old age, and it is miraculous, but do you expect me to believe your story, Mary?" Disbelief, fueled by shame, was turning to anger that threatened to rise within him like a sudden storm on the Sea of Galilee. Joseph could tell by the look of silent pain that crossed her innocent-looking face, that his unusual expression of anger and disbelief had slashed her deeply.

Mary persisted, "But it's true, Joseph. Cousin Elizabeth prophesied by the power of the Holy Spirit about the child I'm carrying—God's Son," Mary pleaded. "She confirmed the angel's message to me, that I was to give birth to Israel's Messiah!"

Joseph sucked in his breath and stood up. What was this? Did he really know Mary? Surely his betrothed was not given to fabricating outrageous stories such as this, yet he didn't know what to make of her words. He knew of Yahweh's prophecies to his people that a messiah would come to deliver Israel, but still… Mary? He sat down, then stood up again, and paced the floor. He put his right hand behind his neck and tilted his head back to relieve a sudden headache.

"I have to go, Mary. I need time to think about what to do," Joseph said. He felt her eyes on his back as he strode across the room, grabbed his cloak by the door, and let himself out.

***

"Yahweh, what am I to do? What has happened to my sweet Mary? Please help me!" Joseph pleaded in prayer as he strode home in anguish. The beautiful furniture he'd made for his Mary seemed to mock him as he opened the door. He could never bring her home as his wife now. What would the neighbors think? His reputation would be ruined, to say nothing of his carpenter business. They'd think he was the father of the child, and that they had… He willed the shameful thought away.

Over the next few days, he threw his energies into making a bench for his neighbor, Matthias, but found it hard to sleep. What should he do about Mary? She was young and perhaps foolish, but he had no wish to shame and disgrace her publicly. That wouldn't be right. He would divorce her quietly—that's what he'd do. After all, divorce was allowed for unfaithfulness. He'd make the arrangements tomorrow.

Decision made, Joseph went to bed early and fell, exhausted, into a deep sleep. As he slept, "an angel of the Lord appeared before him in a dream and said, "Joseph, son of David, do not be afraid to take Mary home as your wife, because what is conceived in her is from the Holy Spirit. She will give birth to a son, and you are to give him the name Jesus, because He will save his people from their sins."[12]

Joseph awoke with a start, and faith stirred and warmed his heart as he carefully considered the angel's words. Mary *had* told him the truth, but he'd judged her so harshly. How must she feel? He turned onto his other side in bed, trying to get comfortable, but his painful thoughts drove him to the decision that he must go see Mary first thing in the morning. He'd bring Mary to his home but wouldn't consummate their marriage until after God's Son was born. He'd bear the gossip and reproach along with her. *Let the neighbors think what they will.* God knew the truth, and that was what mattered most. He would be faithful.

Before the sun made its appearance in a deep blue sky, Joseph had washed and dressed in a long, clean shirt and robe, fastened his sandals, and finished his last bite of breakfast. Throwing his favorite red cloak about his shoulders, he stepped outside, took a deep breath of crisp morning air, and with determined steps, set out to see his betrothed.

---

[12] Matthew 1:20 – 21, NIV

Mary was sweeping the front porch as he approached her house. He saw her look up, and his pace quickened. Mary had never looked more beautiful as she stood still, waiting. He came to her, took the broom from her hands, and set it against the door frame. Without a word, he took her hands into his. She looked deeply into his soul, and the look in her shining eyes spoke volumes. He knew he would always protect and provide for his Mary and her Child, come what may.

Note: I contributed this piece of biblical fiction for an anthology titled *Characters We Know and Love,* in 2016, published by Northern Virginia Christian Writer's Fellowship, of which I am a member. Reprinted by permission of PW Publishing, a division of Portrait Writer, LLC. I own the rights to this story.

Ollie's Legacy

My heart leapt as the auctioneer's fingers dangled an antique heart-shaped locket purse on a metal chain. I remembered that small Mother-of Pearl locket with red lining that opened and snapped shut. Grandma Ollie had kept it in the same dresser drawer as her Amish head coverings, and I used to admire and hold it with care. I knew that on a narrow strip of paper inside the locket, in Ollie's handwriting, were the words, *First gift from my parents, 1903.*

The bidding began as the auctioneer held it aloft, and an antique dealer made a lightning-fast bid. At that moment, something came over me, and I decided I needed to have a little something of my Grandma Ollie's. I counter-bid. The antique dealer bid again, as did I. I determined to have that locket no matter the cost. . .

EARLIER THAT DAY

A feeling of sadness came over me as I drove up the familiar lane alongside the abandoned truck patch and orchard to their "Dawdi" (grandfather) house above the large farmhouse where I and my family once lived. A crowd of people milled about as I found a parking space near the large tent that covered Grandpa Claude's and Grandma Ollie's earthly goods. My Amish Grandma Ollie had been gone for several years, and now Grandpa Claude made sale of their possessions. I couldn't bear the thought of it, nor the throng, so I made my way by foot up their circular driveway to the familiar kitchen door behind the house. An odd feeling came over me as I slowly turned the knob and went inside, thankful to find myself alone.

A lump formed in my throat. In the kitchen, a trio of naked windowsills that once held flowers and cuttings stared blankly at me. I swallowed hard as my eyes moved to the deep kitchen cabinet drawer that once held Ollie's jelly bread treats. I pulled out the drawer as if to catch a whiff of Ollie's bread, then closed it again. I couldn't keep back the tears as I walked to the empty pantry, then wandered back into the bedroom where I used to try on Ollie's Amish head coverings stashed in her top left dresser drawer. Everything seemed so hollow and still.

Away from the din of the auctioneer that yammered mercilessly outside, I made my way to her living room where huge ferns once stood on pedestals between chairs. No begonias filled the four windowsills. Gone was the tall wooden hutch, along with the little yellow plastic chicken that laid plastic eggs when its feet were pushed upwards (a favorite toy of mine). It was always kept in the top right-hand drawer.

Heart heavy with tears, I walked into the dining room and glanced at the bottom step below the door that led to the upstairs. That bottom step always intrigued me as a child. On impulse, I lifted the hinged stair step that formed a neat toy box for us grandchildren. Empty. The spot below two dining room windows was also empty; I wondered who'd bought her treadle sewing machine. Antique dealers, no doubt. The dining room table, glass hutch, and buffet were gone, too.

Resentment pinched.

Badly scuffed floors looked up at me, cracked and wrinkled from age and wear, and my heart ached with sorrow as I returned their dull gaze.

I exited the dining room door onto the large front porch that now sagged and noticed the crumbling concrete steps that led to the yard below. No pots of geraniums graced the porch. No coat of fresh paint comforted the miserable railing.

I made my way gingerly down the crumbling steps and finally positioned myself to see the auctioneer. I watched as boxes of Ollie's dishes, kitchen gadgets, and cookware made their way to hands of strangers.

My thoughts rebelled at such injustice.

As I watched the departure of Ollie's earthly goods, my childhood memories remained. . .

REMEMBERING VISITS TO GRANDMA'S HOUSE

As I knocked on her kitchen door, Grandma Ollie opened it, and her eyes squinted almost shut from the warm smile she gave me. I entered her small but tidy kitchen, and her round face beamed with delight as my brothers followed me inside. Not only did I enjoy the warmth of her personality, but I also enjoyed what I knew was in the deep cabinet drawer by the sink: a loaf of her homemade bread and rich, yellow sour cream butter bought from a neighbor's farm, as well as Ollie's homemade strawberry jam.

Ollie opened the drawer and took out the anticipated treats and generously spread a thick slice for me and my brothers. I enjoyed every bite and licked some jam from the corner of my mouth as I studied her neat appearance: hair parted down the center with the length pulled back into a bun above the nape of her neck. An Amish white head covering, made of starched, white, semi-sheer material, crowned her head. She'd tucked the ends of her covering strings into the neck opening of her blue broadcloth homemade dress. (The only time she tied the strings into a neat little bow was when she and Grandpa Claude went to church on Sundays.) Over the dress, in Amish style, she wore a white cape and apron. In true Amish fashion, she also wore black stockings and two-inch chunky-heeled black shoes that tied.

My eyes took in the various plants on her three sunny kitchen windowsills: cat and kittens, Aloe Vera and begonias, with geranium and rose cuttings in jars of water. The small cloth-covered kitchen table had a second smaller square of cloth draped over salt and pepper shakers, vitamin pills, and other things they used at each meal.

She saw to it that we grandchildren never left her house without a Christian tract. Granted, some terrified my ten-year-old mind. One described the evils of playing cards and the terrors that befell one for doing so. But she gave us good tracts too, that spoke of Jesus and salvation. She let us know her daily prayers centered on our spiritual welfare. I sensed she wished we'd go to their Amish church, but my parents joined the Mennonites when I was just a toddler. And even though we had a more liberal dress code than Grandma Ollie and didn't see eye to eye on some things, I knew she loved us unconditionally.

Her treadle sewing machine below the double dining room windows fascinated me. Seldom idle, it seemed always open with a project in progress—whether it was Amish prayer coverings, men's suits, clothing for herself, shirts for Grandpa Claude, or various hassocks she sold.

She told me of greeting cards she sent to the sick or discouraged, wrote letters of encouragement to prisoners, and penned poetry from her soul. I wish I had some of her writings.

Ollie's generosity, wonderful hospitality, and good cooking were well-known. She kept a well-stocked pantry next to the kitchen, and in the basement rows of wooden shelves held canned goods from her garden as well as canned beef and chicken from the farm. She also made homemade lye soap to use in her wringer washing machine.

CHRISTMAS MEMORIES

I have poignant memories of Christmases at Ollie's house. I loved to organize us grandchildren to put on a Christmas play. We sang songs, recited poems and scripture we had used in our church Christmas programs. Our audience of ten adults sat around the dining room table laden with homemade popcorn balls, "Grandma candy" (penuche peanut fudge), tangerines, and other goodies. Ollie's face beamed as we performed, and all the adults smiled their encouragement for the timid.

A large archway opening between the kitchen and dining room served as our stage, and a bedspread, fastened by large safety pins to a wire stretched across the opening, served as our curtain. Of course, as characters we wore bathrobes and fastened bath towels around our heads with safety pins for an authentic look.

Ollie usually gave me an additional Christmas gift of a serving dish, sugar and creamer set, or other glassware. I still have them today, almost sixty years later. Nostalgia comes over me as I hold the dishes she once gave. She loved pretty dishes and had a glass hutch in the dining room where she displayed her beautiful dinnerware and serving bowls.

SPIRITUAL INTUITION

One day after I'd made a trip to Grandma's house on an errand, she walked back down the lane with me to our house to help my mom. I can still see us together in that lane as she turned to me and softly asked, "Elaine, you've become a Christian, haven't you?" Totally taken by surprise, I privately wondered how she could possibly have known. But I simply replied, "Yes, I have." Ollie replied, "I could tell," and gave me a warm smile that made happy circles go 'round in my heart.

As we continued our walk, I thought back to the Sunday morning it happened, and how I made my profession of faith public at the age of eleven. I had listened to a broadcast of The Radio Kids Bible Class with J.C. Brumfield while the rest of my family finished getting ready for church. The message of the story presented pierced my heart by the convicting power of the Holy Spirit, and I took Jesus as my Lord and Savior. But I had been too timid to tell anyone what I did. Too timid, that is, until later that summer.

Heart pounding, I had stood to my feet at the end of a church bench where I'd sat for the message of the evening during our week-long revival services. I stood and acknowledged to all that I had made Jesus Christ the Lord and Savior of my life. The world just felt right, and I was so happy! I pondered if perhaps Grandma Ollie had seen a change in my countenance or demeanor, or how she could tell I was a Christian. I never asked her. I realized that just because I was raised in a Christian home, went to church every Sunday, was an obedient child and a relatively "good" person and wore a Mennonite head covering didn't mean I was righteous in the sight of God.

DICKY BIRD

Ollie's pet parakeet, Dicky Bird, lived in a cage by the double dining room windows next to her treadle sewing machine. On one of our "jelly bread" visits, I and my brothers gathered around his cage to admire him. I pinched off a bit of my jelly bread and offered it to him, just as Grandma Ollie said, "Now, don't give him any jelly bread; it could hurt him. He eats bird seed." I had already fed him but didn't say anything. I found out some days later that Dickie Bird had died. We grandchildren were standing in her dining room as Grandma Ollie asked, "Did anyone give Dickie Bird some jelly bread?" The solemn silence that followed was broken by me when I timidly said, "I did." Ollie quietly said, "Thank you for being honest, Elaine." She never scolded me. Her kind forgiveness made a huge impression on my young mind. (I have since learned that Dickie Bird likely died of other causes, and not from the jelly bread.)

PRAYER POWER

A devout woman of prayer, Grandma Ollie often said she prayed for us every day, and indeed, the atmosphere around her life was one of holy prayer. I'll never forget a time when she prayed with me in our farmhouse.

Early one morning, my dad and brothers had traveled thirty-some miles to bale hay. In late afternoon, the sky turned black with angry clouds that loomed overhead. Thunder boomed, and lightning flashed close to earth. I think Mom was in the barn, preparing to milk the cows. I was very afraid for the safety of my family, who, by this time, would be traveling home from the distant hayfield. I was also concerned that the baled hay not become wet, because it would become moldy and unfit for cattle consumption. I knelt on our dining room floor beside a chair I'd pulled out and began to pray for their safety and for protection for the hay that it not be soaked by the impending rain. I cried as I prayed. Suddenly, Grandma Ollie appeared! She pulled out a chair and knelt beside me. She prayed silently with me as we knelt together there on the dining room floor, in a spot that became as sacred as the imprint it left on my heart. Just as we finished praying, I heard the tractors come up the road. I stood up, and saw my dad and brothers bring home wagonloads of hay, just in time to avoid the heavy rain that fell later. I don't remember how they got the hay under cover or unloaded in time. Perhaps they threw tarps over the hay wagons, but it never got soaked.

OTHER STORIES OF OLLIE

Every summer, Grandma Ollie helped Mom and me can fruits and vegetables, and as we worked, we talked about all sorts of things, like recipes, women stuff, family stories and community activities. These times further cemented bonds of friendship, respect, and a feeling of belonging.

Mom always spoke well of her mother-in-law and, since Ollie was not one to talk about herself, Mom told me how teenagers at Ollie's church loved to visit her home. More than one night, a young dating couple sneaked into their unlocked house and raided her refrigerator. Ollie heard them and just smiled to herself as she lay in bed, contented.

I also learned that Grandma Ollie taught the women's Bible class at their Amish church on Sunday mornings.

My mom told me about a time Ollie handled keen disappointment. One evening Ollie had guests for dinner, and as Ollie lifted a lemon meringue pie out of the fridge for dessert, it slipped out of her hands, and landed upside down on the kitchen floor! Dessert was ruined. Ollie didn't say a word; she began to hum a song, just scooped up the pie and cleaned up the mess. That made quite an impression on me. Let me assure you, I could not picture myself with such virtue. I never even heard Grandma Ollie utter one angry word, and never knew her to hold a grudge against anyone.

I treasured those stories about Ollie, and I loved her even more.

LIFE CHANGES

But times and seasons change. I graduated from high school, and because of my dad's heart condition, we moved off the dairy farm, away from my beloved Ollie, to a grain farm about twenty miles away. I dated the guy who is now my husband and got a job in a shirt factory in town. My dad's sister's husband and family moved into *my* farmhouse. I rarely got to see Ollie anymore, except for Thanksgiving and Christmas, until it became too much for her.

I got married and started a family of my own. Sad to say, my contact with Grandma Ollie became even less. When she suffered a stroke, I helped take care of her for a few days at her house when I was needed and able to do so. When she passed away a couple of years later, it seemed unreal to me, and I felt a keen sense of loss, like I'd missed some very important years of her life.

THE LOCKET AND LEGACY

And now, as the auctioneer held Ollie's precious locket aloft, and the antique dealer bid again, I swiftly raised my card again to indicate a higher bid. After a few more times of back and forth, he suddenly stopped bidding. I had won my prize! I paid forty dollars for that little heart-shaped purse locket—a little bit of Ollie I could hold in my hands.

I wish I could reach out and hug my Grandma Ollie. I don't remember ever doing that, nor do I remember being hugged. But her kind words, her manner of including me with the women folk in their conversation and activities, her eyes when she looked at me, her laughter that squeezed them tightly shut, spoke volumes to me. I don't think the Amish gave displays of affection, but that's okay. They did the best they knew with how they'd been taught.

Today, much like my Grandma Ollie, I love to send letters and cards to the sick and discouraged. I have written to two prisoners for several years. I have published three children's books and a cookbook, a devotional book, written poetry, and taught Bible classes. I've had a sewing business doing alterations, making bridal apparel and even two Amish men's suits. I used to watch her bake cinnamon rolls and bread, and now I bake them.

One may forget what someone says, but one never forgets how they made you feel. And when I think of Grandma Ollie, I feel unconditionally loved! Even though she never published a book, she wrote one on my heart.

Note: I contributed this piece for an anthology titled *Legacy: Heartprints that Linger,* in 2018, published by Northern Virginia Christian Writer's Fellowship, of which I am a member. Reprinted by permission of PW Publishing, a division of Portrait Writer, LLC. I own the rights to this work.

A Touch of Eden

The sunset is a bright copper shimmer through a copse of dark evergreens as I step onto the deck and sit in my favorite spot. Across the way, the windows of a row of townhouses facing west are turned to sheets of gold. The pale blue expanse above the pines is awash with color: golds, pinks, reds, oranges, and lavenders with a slice of lemon here and there.

I draw a deep breath and let my body relax as my eyes drink in the kaleidoscope of color before me. A gentle breeze cools my flushed face and pleasantly-tired limbs as I lock my hands behind my head and put up my feet. I imagine myself in the color-drenched canopy overhead, being the tiny puff of a cloud slowly carried along by gentle currents as a silver jet plane streaks a white banner by me.

Newly-budding tips of two oak trees are swaying like a hula dancer in the warm air, made fragrant by my freshly-mown lawn. On the gold-tinted grassy carpet lie several handfuls of last year's dead oak trees that don't all shed until the new life in spring thrusts them off. The branches hold out their lacy fingertips to receive the sun's benediction.

A few birds chirp faintly to each other as they prepare to nest for the night. A screen door squeaks, and a neighbor's child steps into the twilight, skipping happily to a swing for one last fling at play before bedtime. The distant throaty roar of a motorcycle makes me smile as I imagine the rider also thrilling to this special time of day. Nearby, a dog barks his delight.

In the stratosphere on a patch of deepening blue, the planet Venus appears, bright with glory. A bat feeding on the wing swoops in curves across the now mostly-gray clouds, darting silently, graceful and carefree. The distant mountain range is cloaked in a mystery of purple as dusk steals gently upon me as softly as a blanket is tenderly placed on a sleeping child.

The balmy evening air caresses my face, and I am moved to worship God—to be in awe of the splendor of His creation, and to listen for His voice in my spirit. And I think of Eden.

How God must have enjoyed friendship with Adam and Eve in the cool of the day when the world was young! I wonder if the same breeze that now touches my cheek may have played across the faces of earth's first man and woman one night many years ago.

I bow my head and pray, grateful to God for my life and the peace in my heart despite our upside-down culture, political corruption, violence that fills our land and cries of the oppressed. I think of a poem I once wrote:

> O Eagle of the mountain heights,
> Wings once outstretched in noble flight,
> Who dimmed your eye, once keen and bright,
> And caged you 'round with blackest night?

Tears sting my eyes as I whisper the desire in my heart: "Your kingdom come, Your will be done, on Earth, as it is in heaven."[13] And I long for Eden.

---

[13] Matthew 6:10

Printed in the United States
By Bookmasters